Ready to befriend Afraid!

Tap the lid twice to open the jar
and then turn the page.

YIKES!!
Afraid is freaking out!

3

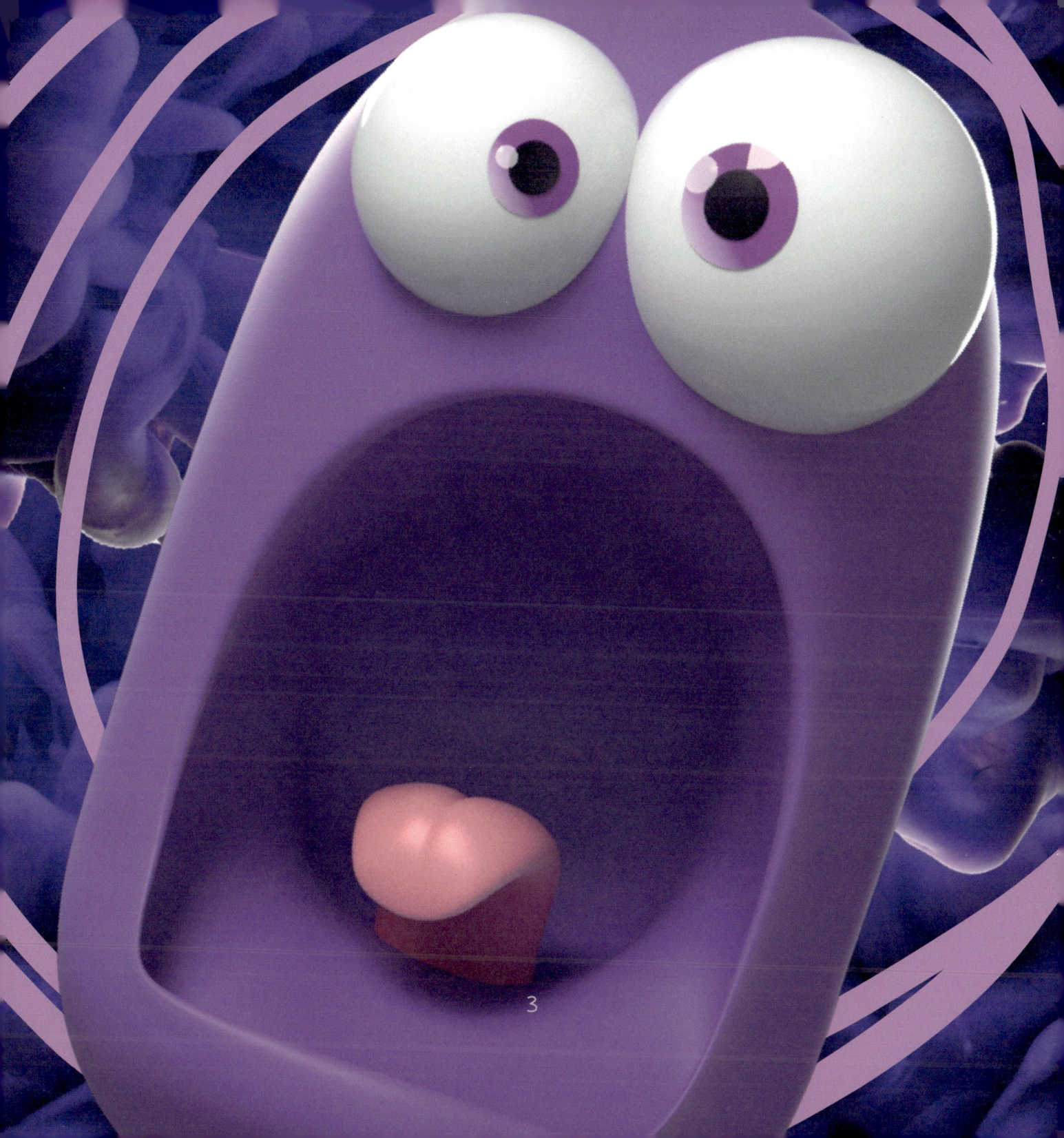

Quick! Pound on the ice with your fist to break your breath free.

Then turn the page.

YOUR
BREATH

GREAT WORK!

Now help Afraid take a deep breath in, just like this.

YOUR BREATH

Close your eyes
and blow the air out
as slowly as you can

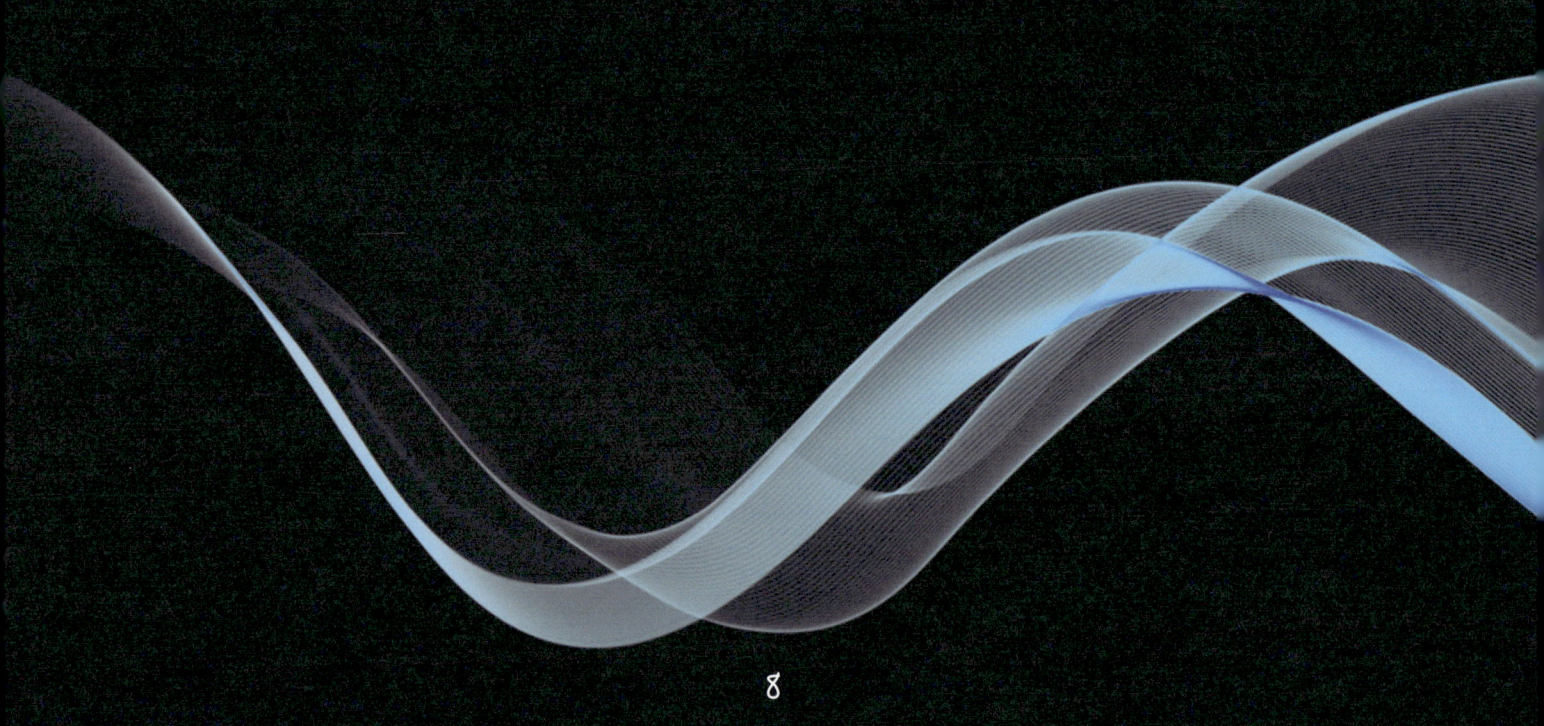

WHOOOOSH

wee!

10

Do you feel a
little better?

No? Maybe turning
on the lights will help.

Use your finger
to flip the switch.

14

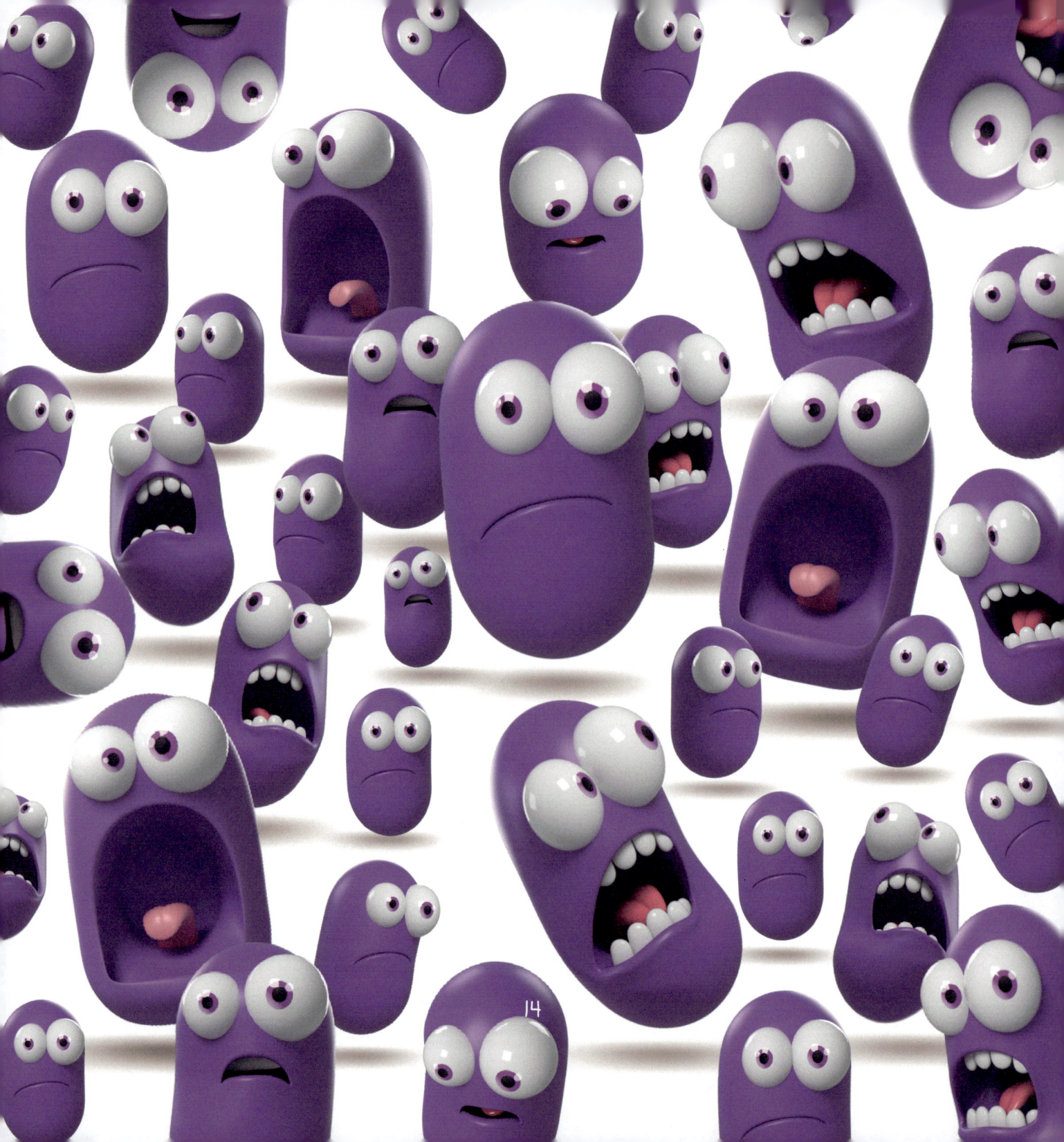

WHOA.

Afraid multiplied!

16

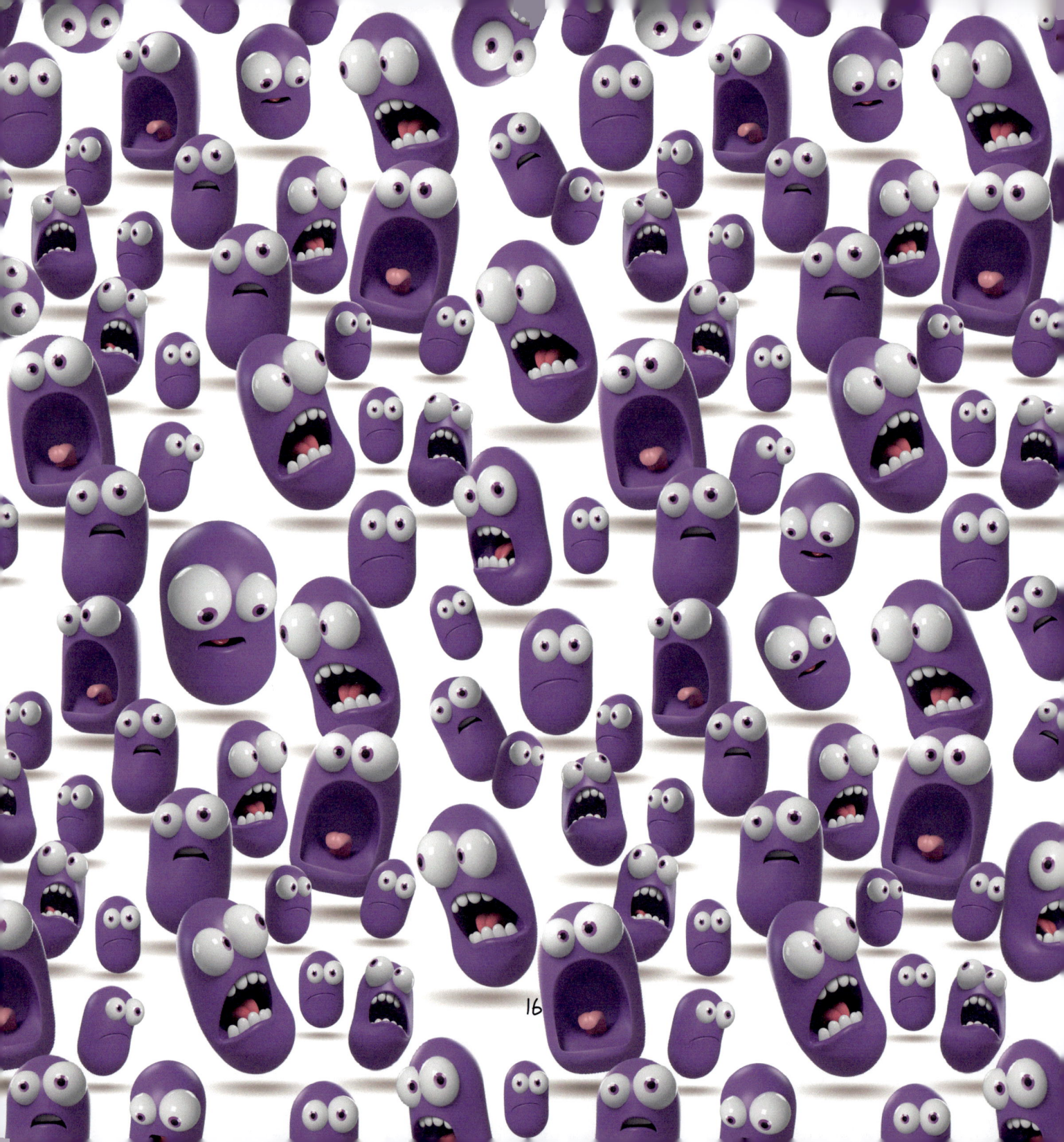

And KEEPS multiplying!

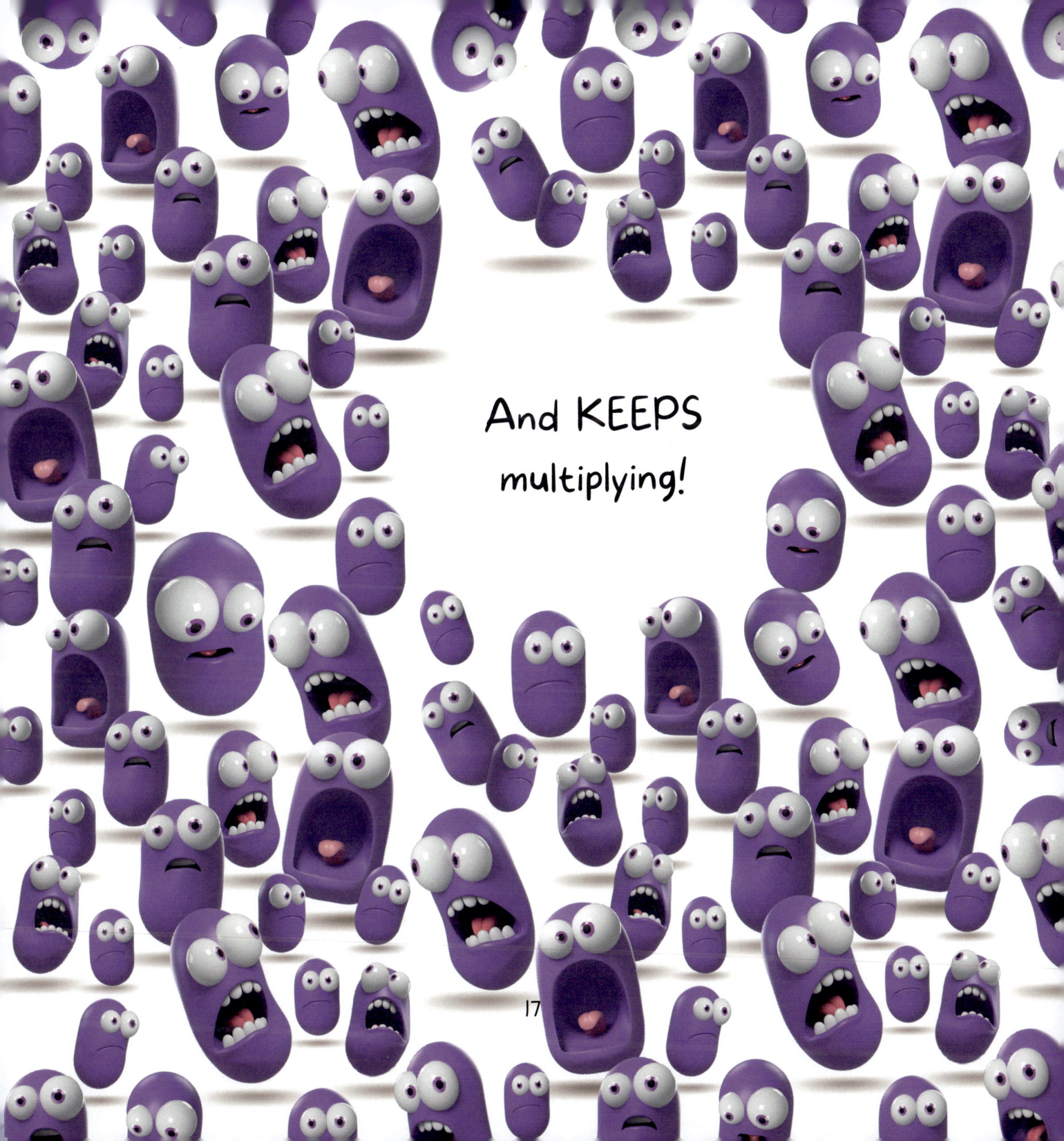

When Afraid multiplies, the first thing to ask yourself is:

Am I safe?

(Like – is a tiger about to eat you?)

If so...

You could scream and

RUN!!

(maybe use a catapult if you have one)

Or you could
get very still

and hide, like you were
frozen in an ice cube.

If a tiger ISN'T about to eat you, then you probably don't have to run or hide.

Instead, it's time to listen.

What is your fear
asking you to do?

27

Is it asking you to pay
closer attention to something?

29

Or gather
more information?

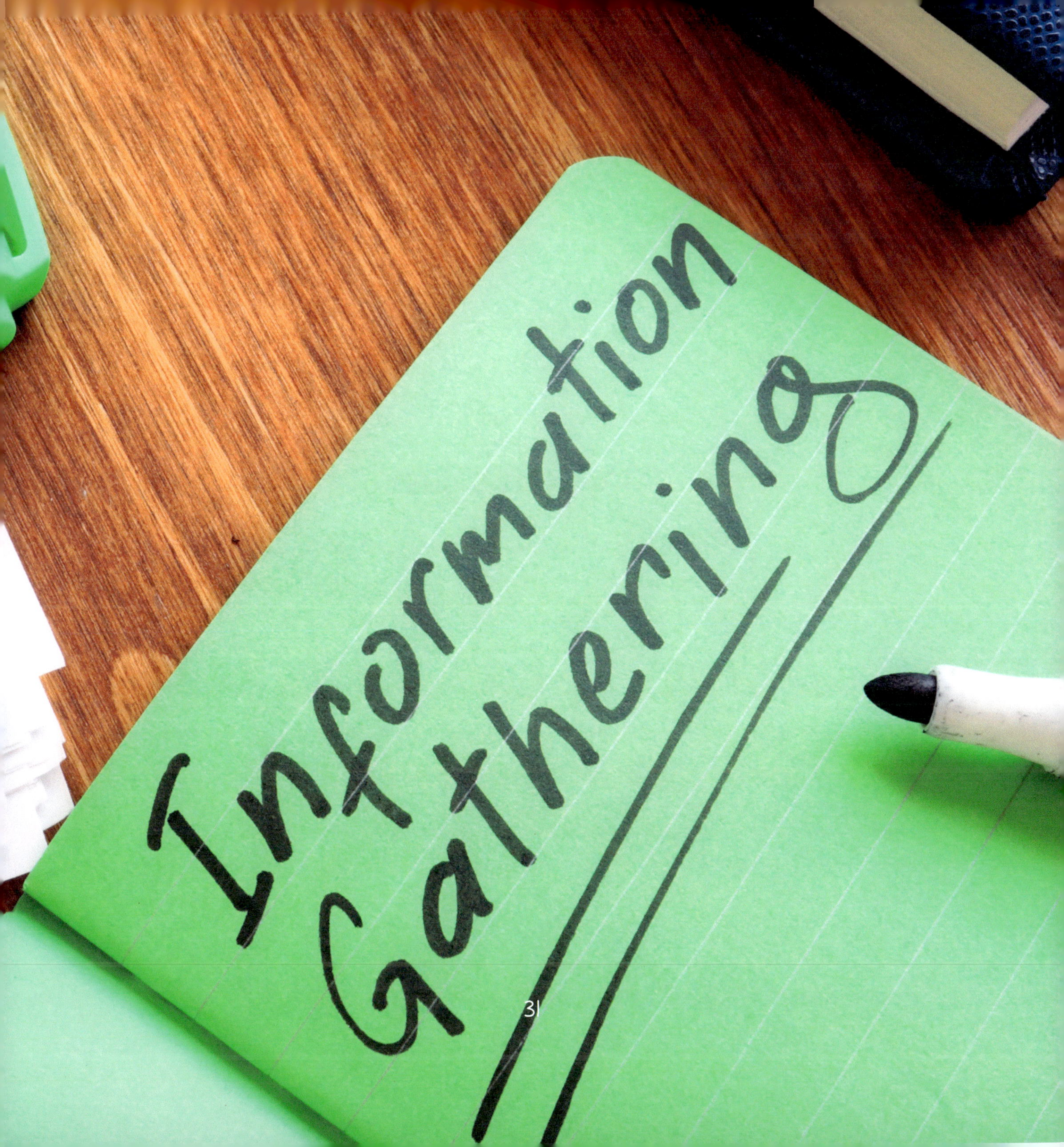
Information
Gathering

Maybe it's just
telling you to slow down.

33

If you listen carefully, you will know why Afraid is here.

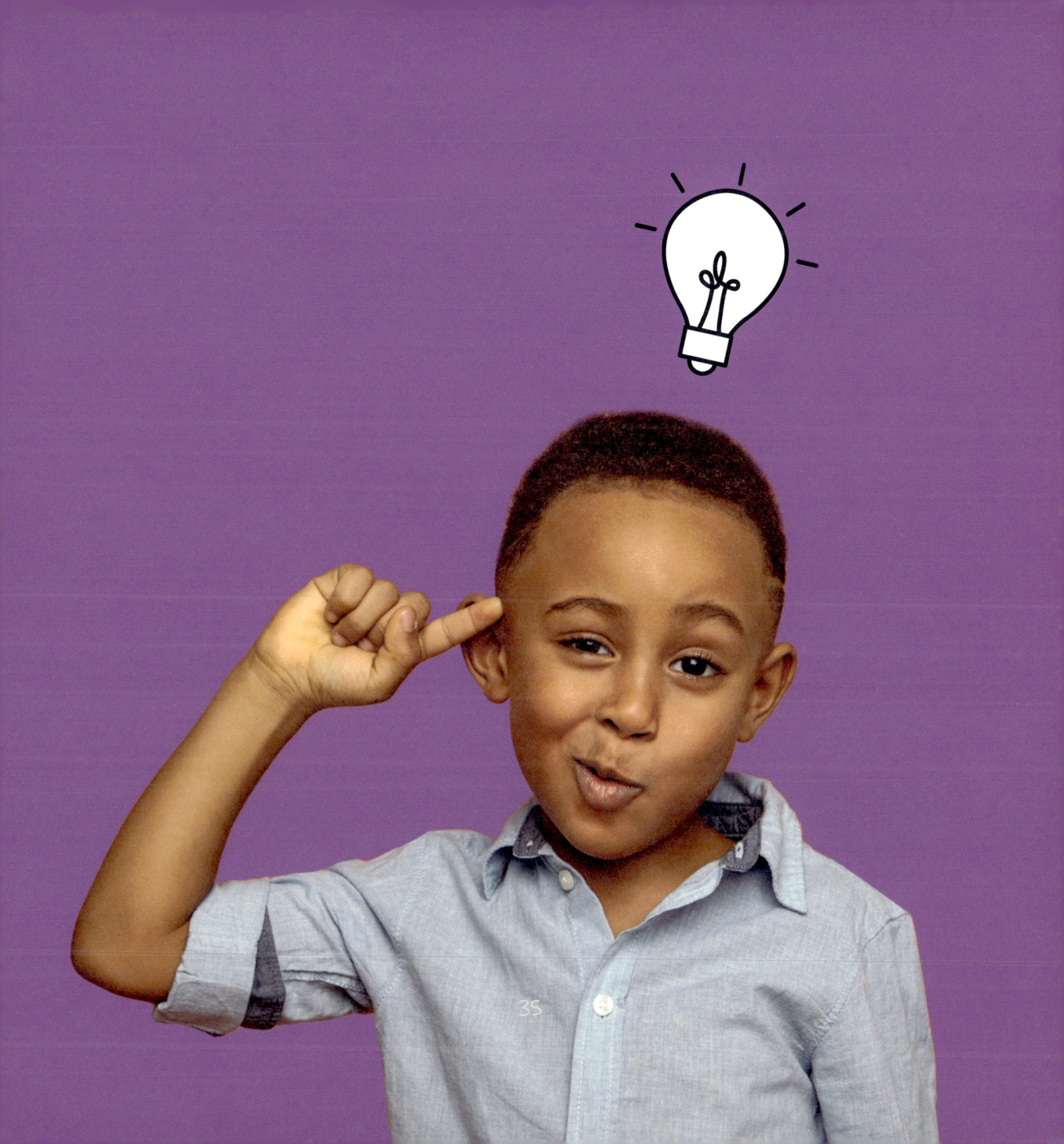

Trust yourself.

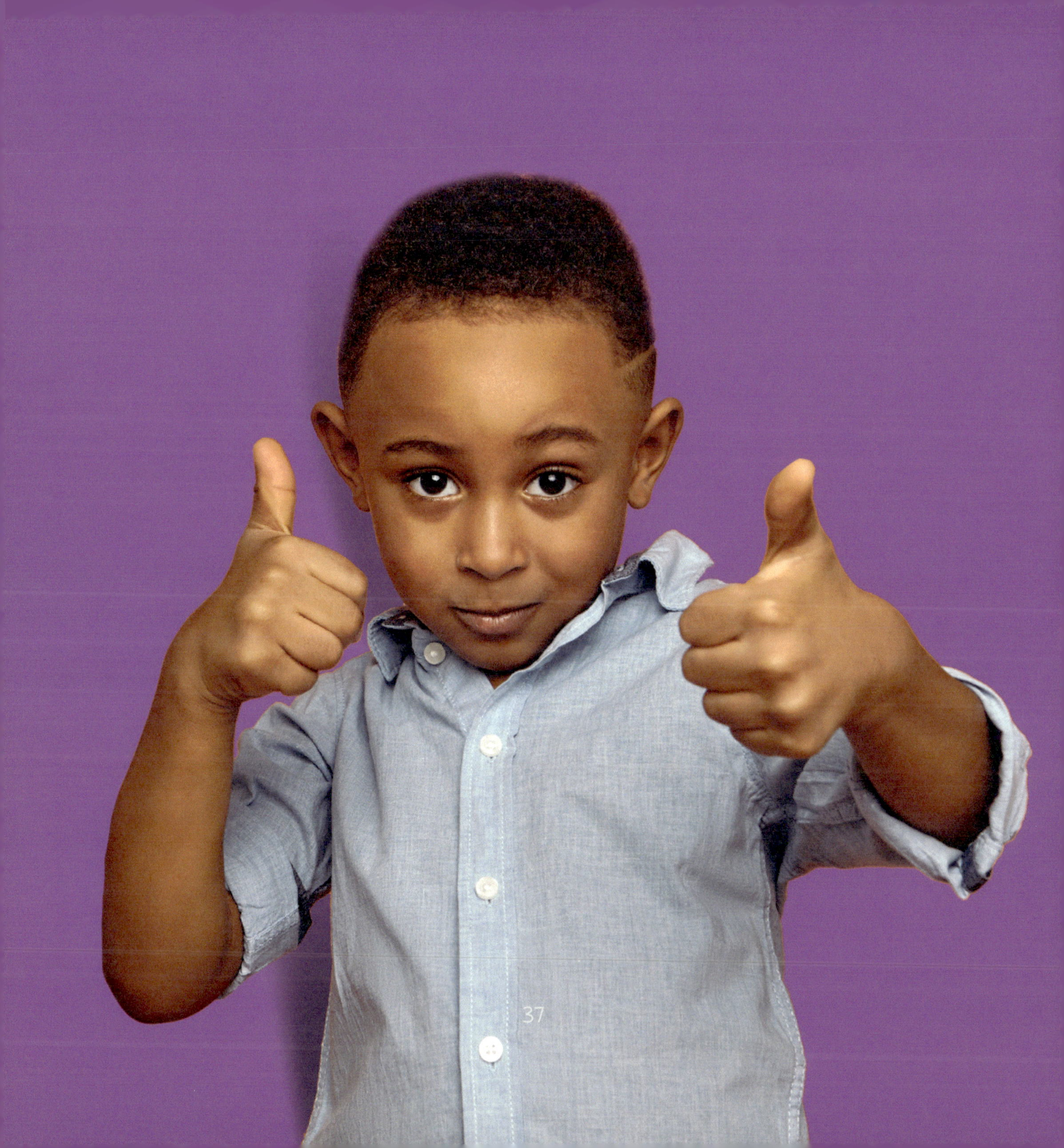

This is how Afraid can turn into COURAGE.

COURAGE CAN HELP YOU

- say "no"
- ask for help
- try something new
- face a big challenge

No matter what this feeling is asking you to do, remember that you don't have to do it all at once.

Save Money

it HAPPEN

Less Time on Internet

Get Fit

Walk

You just have to pay attention to
THIS MOMENT. RIGHT NOW.

(Use your finger to trace the
line as you take **3** deep breaths)

BREATHE IN
BREATHE IN
BREATHE IN

START

BREATHE OUT
BREATHE OUT
BREATHE OUT

Wow. Your breath is POWERFUL!
It made the heart grow bigger. ⟹

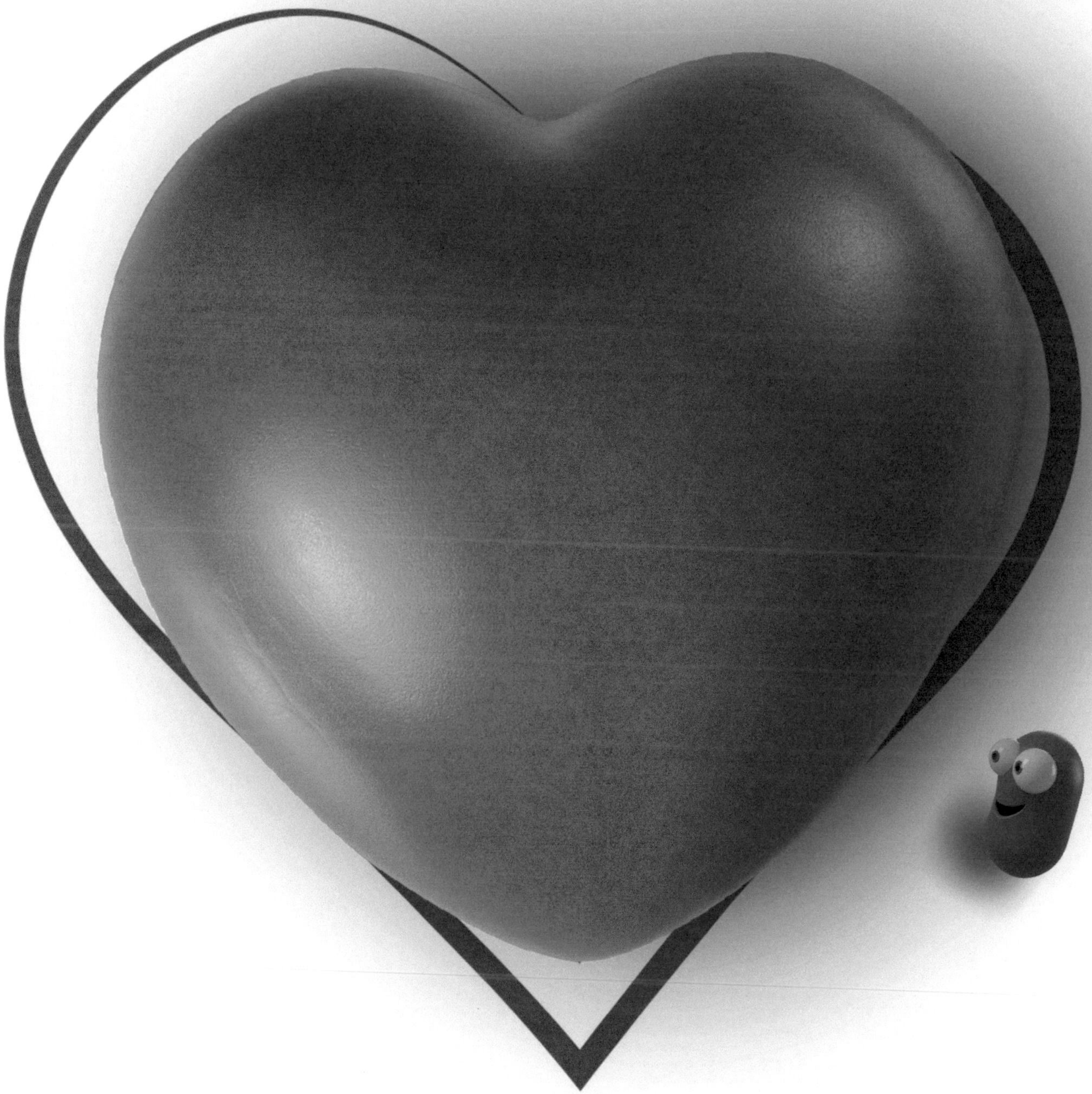

Oooh!
What's happening now?

47

A door opened!
And Courage is climbing in!

49

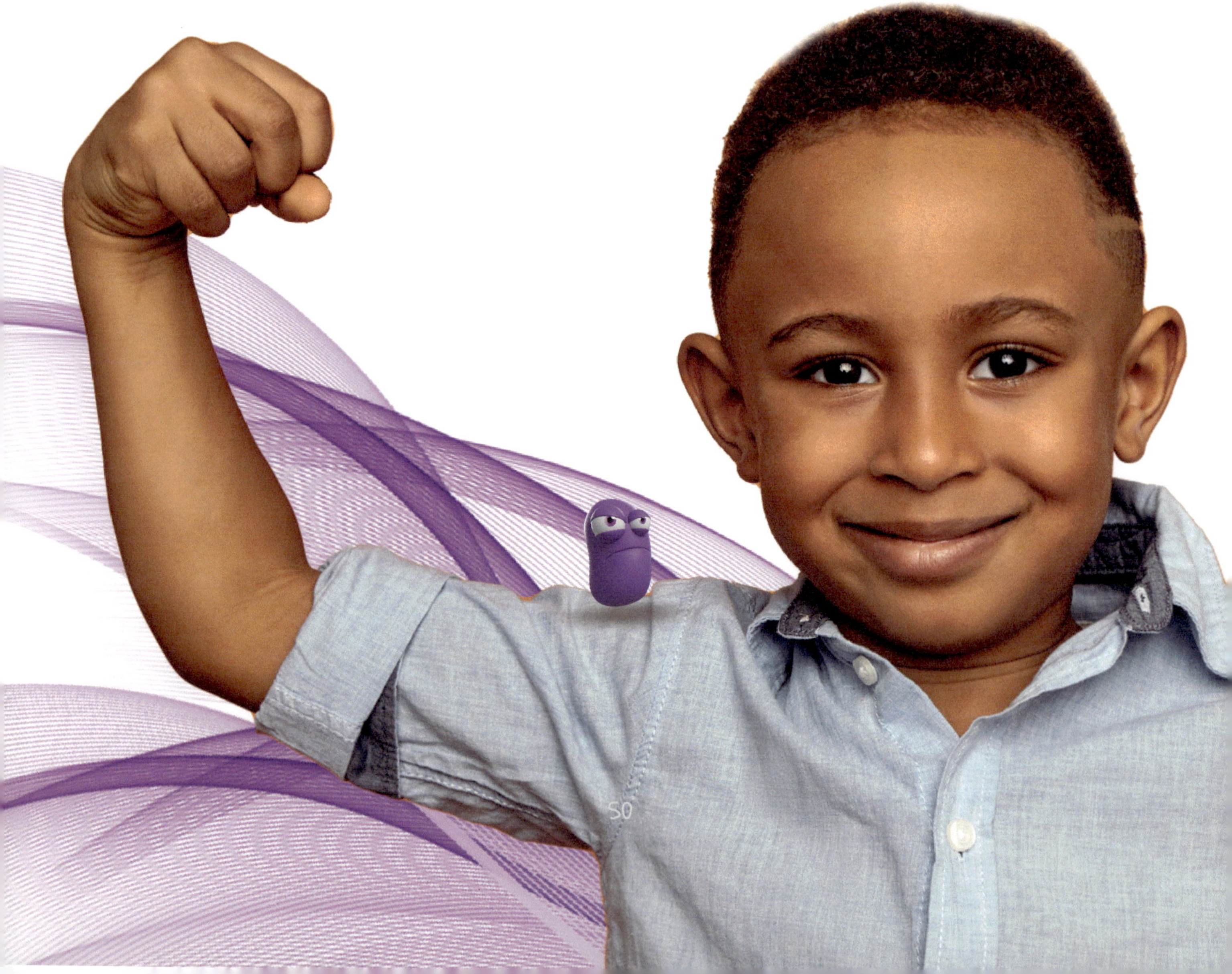

With Courage in your Heart

you can trust yourself to find your strength, one breath at a time.

Beautiful Work!

Read this book whenever Afraid is visiting and you want to learn more about this emotion.

Use pens, pencils, and crayons
to fill out the next few pages.

| Rapid Heartbeat | Mind Racing | Cold Sweat | Goose-bumps |

| Trembling or Tingling | Hard to Breathe |

When Afraid Comes to Visit, Your Body Gives You Clues

Which clues apply to you?

| Chills or Body Aches | Dry Mouth or Nausea |

| Dizziness or Trouble Focusing | Blurred Vision or Narrowed Focus |

WORRIED　　ANXIOUS　　AFRAID　　OVERWHELMED　　PANICKED

CAN YOU GIVE YOUR AFRAID FEELING A NAME?

54

What does your afraid feeling look like?

Use this space to draw it:

What Are You Going to Do With Afraid? Are You Ready To Make a Sunshine Choice?

Before you take action, make sure your choice is:

✓ Respectful
✓ Responsible
✓ Kind

Choices that are respectful, responsible and kind are called "Sunshine Choices" because they feel warm in your heart like sunshine... and help you be your best self.

POSSIBLE SUNSHINE CHOICES:

- Get Away from Danger
- Face Something Scary
- Get Curious & Ask Questions
- Ask For Help
- Develop A New Skill
- Make A Plan
- Pay Close Attention to Something New
- Find Your Strength
- Take Some Deep Breaths

MAKE SUNSHINE CHOICES LIKE MAYA & BECOME A WIGGLE WARRIOR®

WHEN I'M FEELING MAD

WHEN I'M FEELING ICKY

WHEN I'M FEELING SAD

WHEN I'M FEELING AFRAID

I CHOOSE TO BE BRAVE

I CHOOSE TO BE RESILIENT

I CHOOSE TO BE HONEST

I CHOOSE TO BE ASSERTIVE

©Anne Kubitsky

MAKE A SUNSHINE CHOICE

MAD
I CHOOSE TO CALMLY STATE MY NEEDS

ICKY
I CHOOSE TO BE HONEST + ASK FOR HELP

GLAD
I CHOOSE TO BE CALM + CURIOUS + KIND

AFRAID
I CHOOSE TO BE BRAVE + TRY NEW THINGS

SAD
I CHOOSE TO SLOW DOWN + CARE FOR MYSELF

ANNE KUBITSKY
Author, Illustrator & Book Designer

Anne is the Founder & CEO of Look for the Good Project, Inc. She has received numerous awards for her innovative efforts to create social change, including the "Points of Light Award" - a community service award originating out of The White House. She holds a dual degree in biology and philosophy from Smith College, with additional undergraduate and graduate training in graphic design, illustration, and art education. Anne has been studying meditation, yoga, spirituality, psychology, and a variety of therapeutic models for over 20 years. Look for the Good Project is her effort to support the larger community with the healing tools she has discovered along the way. Anne is donating 100% of the proceeds from this book to Look for the Good Project. Please visit **lookforthegoodproject.org** to learn more about Anne's Wiggle Warrior® book series.

ADDITIONAL ILLUSTRATION CREDITS

Special thanks to ANMP, a group of talented artists in Europe who have collectively worked on a variety of well known films: *Maleficent*, *Loki*, *Wonder Woman 1984*, *The Lion King*, and *The Witches*. With Anne serving as Art Director, ANMP helped Anne animate some of her Wiggle Warrior® characters which you can see online. Thanks also to Axel Blin for his stellar animation skills, and Song Na for his human character designs (bravo!).

MENTAL HEALTH REFERENCES

A lot of research went into developing these concepts. To learn more, check out:

Therapeutic Models
- Internal Family Systems (IFS)
- Somatic Internal Family Systems
- AEDP Therapy
- Somatic Experiencing (SE)
- Applied Polyvagal Theory

Trauma Psychoeducation
Linda Thai's Certificate in Somatic Embodiment & Regulation Strategies

Child Development
The Center on the Developing Child at Harvard University & The Attachment Project

Some Great Experts in the Field

Linda Thai, LMSW
Dr. Arielle Schwartz
Dr. Nadine Harris
Pete Walker, MA
Dr. Carol S. Dweck
Dr. Peter Levine
Dr. Gabor Maté

Deb Dana, LCSW
Dr. Frank Anderson
Dr. Brené Brown
Dr. Christina Reese
Dr. Emily Nagoski
Dr. Barbara Fredrickson
Dr. Bruce D. Perry

Karla McLaren, M.Ed
Dr. Judson Brewer
Dr. Bessel van der Kolk
Dr. Janina Fisher
Stanley Rosenberg
Dr. Stephen Porges
Susan McConnell

If you are a grown-up, Anne's workbook **Time to Shine** is an excellent first step in learning more about emotions, how to process them, and how to better attune to the children in your life.

Special thanks to our Sunshine Friend Gaye Pigott

for caring so much about the wellbeing of school communities, and for generously nurturing the development of our Wiggle Warrior® Program.

This book was created in loving memory of

Ruth Robins, Debbie Goodrow and Edna & Doug Noiles

SUNSHINE FRIENDS:

- Are consistently kind to you
- Make you feel calm & safe
- Are warm and nurturing (like sunshine!)
- Respect your boundaries
- Are concerned about your wellbeing
- Are supportive when you're struggling
- Make you feel seen, understood & appreciated
- Never try to hurt you
- Are not jealous of your joy and know how to celebrate your achievements
- Love you just as you are
- Apologize for their mistakes and do things to fix them
- Are interested in earning your trust

READY FOR MORE?

To learn about our Wiggle Warrior® Program, or to access free content online, please visit our website: **lookforthegoodproject.org**

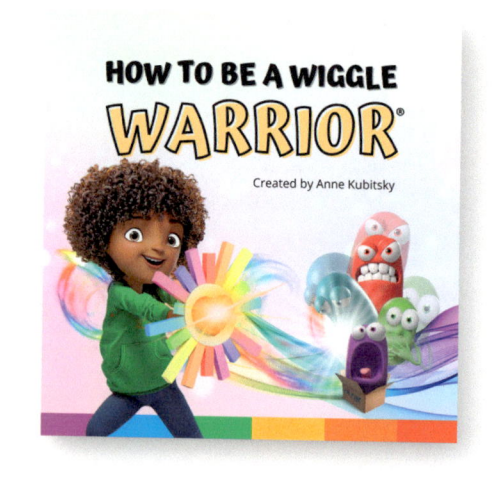

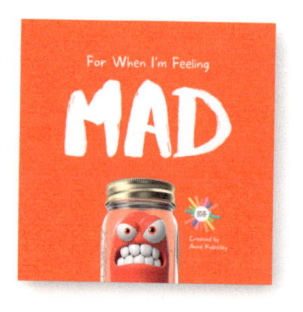

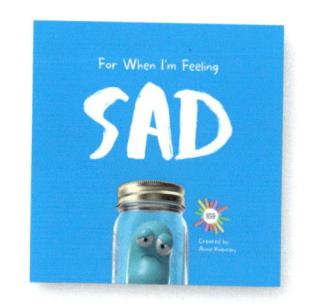

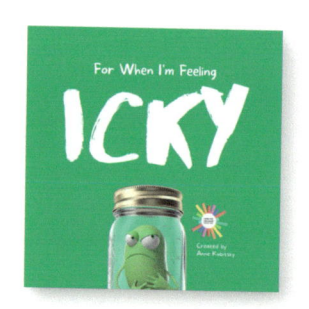

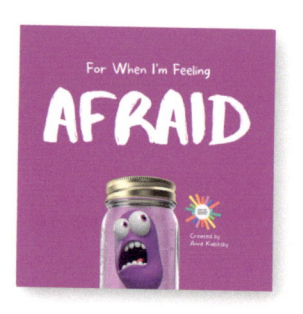

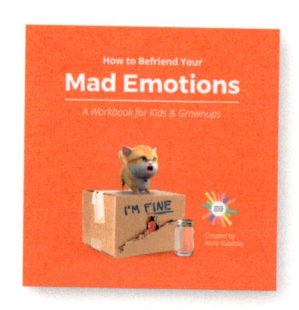

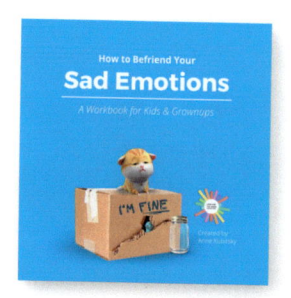

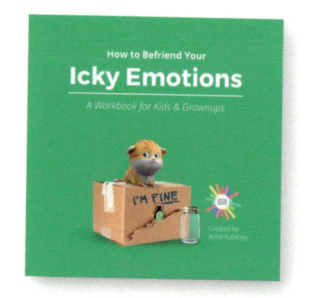

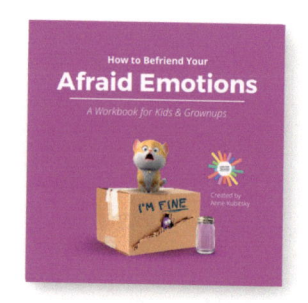

Grow through
what you go through.

Wiggle Warrior® Books
An imprint of Look for the Good Project, Inc.
Text copyright © 2021 by Anne Kubitsky. Illustrations and photographs owned or licensed by Anne Kubitsky. All rights reserved. No part of this book may be reproduced, scanned or distributed in any printed or electronic form without permission in writing from the author.
lookforthegoodproject.org

Made in the USA
Columbia, SC
30 November 2024